MW01235066

WILLPOWER

21 STEPS TO DEVELOP SELF DISCIPLINE AND CONTROL

APOSTOLOS GRADALES

Why I Wrote This Book

This book was written to help folks just like you learn methods of molding yourself into someone that can reach multiple levels of success throughout life, no matter the obstacles that stand in your way.

The word 'willpower' is made up of two strong words that when put together, can create a powerful force in changing your life. 'Will' is simply the ability to make choices consciously. We as human beings are creatures with unlimited amounts of will at our disposal. Will is powered by desire, but without the motivation to exercise that will, you would never assert yourself to make decisions that help you to reach your ultimate goals.

Throughout the easy-to-read chapters in this book, you will find ways to change various aspects of your everyday life in such a way that leads you to become a more fruitful individual. This book was written for everyday people looking to improve their willpower to achieve the success they know they are capable of!

Why You Should Read This Book

It's time to really be honest with yourself when it comes to discussing your personal willpower in the midst of everyday living.

- Do you struggle getting motivated to complete tasks?

- Do you find yourself wasting valuable time on your mobile devices?

- Do you have a strong desire to make a difference but aren't sure where to start to achieve this goal?

- Do you have a desire to be able to complete more in a days' time?

- Do you have issues making adequate decisions that will land you farther in obtaining your goals and dreams?

If any of these questions apply to your personal life, then you will benefit greatly from taking the time to read this book. Willpower is not just about having the ability to make hard but needed decisions. It is an aspect of everyday life that has the power to feed into all parts of the way you live. Once you become more seasoned in building up your willpower, you will find that many other areas of your life will become brighter and easier to live.

The following chapters are valuable but are not necessarily written in the order. Each will vary in importance depending on what areas you need to focus on first. Feel free to skip around, but make sure you read them all in their entirety. Read them all, because even the smallest of changes can make a significant difference in your life!

TABLE OF CONTENTS

What Is Willpower?

Willpower is the strength that we all have inside ourselves that provides us with the ability to not only make decisions but also carry them out accordingly. Willpower is the muscle we all need to fight against the inevitable resistance and difficulties that life throws our way. Not to mention those times where we feel too lazy or discomforted to move forward.

Willpower is ultimately the power of pushing yourself in the direction of goals, desires, and achievements. Without it, we would lack in assertiveness, determination, and decisiveness that push us to continue onward.

Believe it or not, willpower is similar to stress when it boils down to how our bodies react. Just like stress, which is not only a psychological phenomenon, willpower is both a mind and bodily experience. While stress is our reaction to external threats, willpower is the response we have to internal conflicts.

Without willpower, we would be like chickens with our head cut off, running around in circles. Willpower enables us to resist temptation and keeps us from acting on urges that are self-destructive. Willpower is responsible for the "pause-and-plan" response, which keeps us in a calm state of mind as we "power" through situations and consider the best options. It also sends energy to our frontal cortex in the brain, which enables us to keep adequate track of goals and oversee cravings or impulses that will unpaved our path to success.

Willpower is all about honing the mindset to have the motivation to do what matters the most in life.

Unfortunately, there are many things we do every day that inhibit our willpower and keep us from obtaining our goals.

- Lack of sleep

- Eating Unhealthy

- Inability to deal and lower stress

- Lack of exercise

- Being unorganized

- Inability to establish everyday routines

- Inability to embrace the power of change

- Lack of focus

- Lack of the bigger picture when it comes to goals

- Etc.

The following chapters will outline and discuss the many aspects of everyday life to have the ability to get in the way of achieving our goals and aspirations. It's time to start making changes in how you perceive and live your life. By the end of this book, you will learn valuable assets in strengthening your willpower and becoming the best version of yourself you can be!

CHAPTER 1. GET A GOOD MORNING ROUTINE.

The entirety of my day seems to go *so* much better when I have started the morning right. My mood, my concentration, my energy, *everything*.

Whether you are a night owl or an early riser, morning routines are crucial in regards to setting the tone for the rest of the day. I will be honest with you; when you have a day that is set up right from the get-go, you are more likely to fulfill the steps needed to achieve success.

Morning routines don't just *happen*; you have to *choose* to take part in them. If you look into the everyday life of prosperous individuals, you will often find that they have established some sort of routine to start out each day, and they are *in love* with them!

THE IMPORTANCE OF A MORNING ROUTINE

"How you start your day is how you start your life" – Drew Canole

GOOD MORNING ROUTINES...

- Help lower stress and promotes relaxation

- Provides the ability to have a sharp and clear mind

- Ability to accomplish more in a day's time

- Higher energy levels

- Overall happier *and* healthier

- Promotes wellbeing and long-term success

- Helps to build momentum to grow as a person

Bad Morning Routines…

- Automatically set you up to have a stress-filled day

- Gives you brain fog, which enables bad decision making

- Enables unhealthy eating habits

- Leads to lethargy due to lack of energy

- Increased levels of depression and anxiety

- Long-term benefits do not exist

- Causes you to remain in the same rut you are in for extended periods of time

CREATING A *GOOD* MORNING ROUTINE

Everyone is different, which means there are a plethora of things you can decide to do to create a morning routine that works well for you personally. There may be some trial and error involved as you build your perfect routine, just be sure that you want your routine to tailor *your* life, not someone else's.

EXAMPLES OF MORNING ROUTINE ACTIVITIES

Be Grateful

Being thankful is an easy action that bestows a lot of power. When you take a few moments our of each day to feel grateful for what you have in life, you're are more apt to see the bigger picture, which fuels success. This can be as simple as looking around you and taking notice of all the things you have in your life. When you wake up and feel powerfully thankful, this can dramatically change your point of view and emotions.

Exercise

Exercise is a very common part of many people's morning routine. There is quite a bit of research to back up the positive effect that exercise has on the body, specifically in the A.M. It gives you a nice boost of mental acuity that can last up to *10 hours*! Think about the things you can accomplish in just a days' time!

Exercise also boosts your metabolic levels, which enables your body to burn more calories so that you can keep that trim body! The goal of exercise in the morning is to reach the level of aerobic effort so that the chemicals in your brain release that lactic acid fogging your mind and produce positive effects throughout your body.

Visualization

This is one of my personal favorite parts of my morning routine. There are many easy visualization practices you can conduct in the A.M. There are many successful folks that simply close their eyes and imagine themselves where they want to be. When you actually see yourself obtaining your goals, your brain then produces the emotions associated with it, creating the motivation to keep moving forward.

Meditation

The act of meditation is often paired greatly alongside visualization. It's way simpler than it sounds too!

- Set a timer for 10 minutes.

- Sit up straight, focusing on your breath coming and leaving your body. Do this till the timer goes off.

It's that simple! Be prepared for your mind to wander as you perform this activity. The entire goal of meditation is learning how to bring yourself back slowly to the present with each breath. Meditation takes practice, but when combined with visualization, it can be a mighty reassurance that you are well on your way to achieving those aspirations!

Drinking Water

Did you know that consuming water immediately after waking up has substantial benefits? If these don't make you want to put some water on your bedside table, I don't know what will!

- Rehydrates the body

- Flushes toxins

- Boosts metabolism

- Fuels the brain

- Relieves constipation

- Cures and prevents diseases

- Makes the consumer feel refreshed!

Goal Setting

Don't overcomplicate this activity, for it's as easy as it sounds. Take a few minutes during your morning to set goals for what you wish to accomplish for that particular day. This will help to establish the goals you want for your life.

Avoid These Morning Activities

- Checking email

- Hitting the snooze button repeatedly

Positive changes only happen when the foundation is set with positive changes; it goes hand in hand! It takes just one positive change to set the tone for establishing more changes that will lead you on the path to ultimate success.

I challenge you to look at the list of activities in this chapter. Over this next week, try each one on different mornings. When you find the one you like, create a unique morning routine that is based on your preferences and needs.

Many of the above activities will be discussed deeper in the following chapters!

CHAPTER 2. GET ORGANISED

There is always that one person at the office that has papers, folders, knick-knacks, writing utensils and God knows what else on their desk. Nothing is organized, and things are scattered everywhere. While some people are successful and disorganized, more often than not, these two words usually never pair well together.

A big part of willpower is becoming organized to such a degree that you can eliminate useless stress. This helps you to maintain a low level of brain fog and focus on what is really important.

HEALTH BENEFITS OF BEING ORGANIZED

There are some of us who would rather watch a Netflix marathon or read a book rather than taking the time to reorganize and clean up life. That's why I have placed these amazing benefits of organization here to make you reconsider turning on that television.

BOOSTS ENERGY

Even though organizing sounds like an energy eliminator, it actually is quite the opposite. If you are feeling a bit blue, take a few minutes to organize a work area. This can help you to feel more energetic while doing something drastically positive!

Promotes Healthier Eating Habits

Positive organization has shown to have a direct effect on what we choose to fuel our bodies with. Those who are around and work constantly in a neat environment choose items such as an apple rather than a chocolate bar. If you want to get trimmer for the holidays, then get organized yourself. You will then see yourself consuming much healthier meals.

Improved Sleep

Keeping your life organized can help you fall asleep faster and stay asleep! I know I am one that constantly ponders about the clutter in my bedroom and house when I am trying to get some shut-eye. Learn the importance of a clean living environment when it comes to your overall physical health. You will see the changes in your sleeping habits as you de-clutter your home over time.

Reduces Stress

While stress is an inevitable part of human life, there are many ways we can choose to lessen it. It's been found that those with cluttered-filled home and many unfinished projects are more tired, depressed, and anxious than those that take every day to organize, put-away, and finish projects. The stress hormone cortisol leads to those feeling unhappy in everyday life. Who knew that a little organizing could conquer this?

Lowered Risk of Heart Attack

Stop popping pills and drinking those green drinks and take the time to organize your home and workplace! It has been proven that organization has a direct impact on whether or not you are at a higher risk to experience heart issues. Those that perform regular housecleaning, yard work, and do DIY projects reduce their risk by 30%! If that's not a good excuse, then I don't know what is!

TIPS TO KEEP LIFE ORGANIZED

Even those that already practice healthy organization can gain positive change from some of the following organization tips! There should be a little something for the majority of folks on the following list:

- 3 Important tasks: Write out the three most pertinent tasks that you need to get done. If you have these written down, you are more apt to complete them.

- Easy 'to-do' lists: While there are hundreds of fancy apps that can create a list for you, avoid them. Make a simple list of things you need to complete that day. This way you aren't hunting around on your phone for where you typed things out.

- Choose one tool that gets the job done and stick with it.

- Avoid multitasking. Do one thing at a time.

- Don't put things off. Do them *now*.

- Learn the importance of saying 'no.'

- Utilize the recycling/trash bin: Stop wasting time organizing items that are unnecessary to your success. It's a waste of valuable time.

- Find a place for everything

- Learn to simplify

- Put things away *right* away: Make it a habit of putting things away right when you are done using them. This is efficient and prevents your space from becoming cluttered.

- Divide things into folders: You know those cool colored folders? Go out and get you some! Pick a color to place all the things that need to be done today, use another color for bills, etc.

- Learn to take control of your time and priorities

- Sort at the source: This is one of the most helpful tips in my personal life. I usually take a trip to my post office box 1-2 times a week. Instead of bringing every single piece of mail back to my house, I sort right there, throwing junk mail away, sorting bills, etc.

- Use note cards: Write tasks on note cards. Stack them in order of highest to lowest priority. You can also arrange them on boards, throw them away when done, or reuse them and arrange them differently. An easy-to-carry priority driven to-do list!

- Learn the power of minimalizing your life. Less is more!

- Learn to delegate: Especially in the workplace, learn what people are best at and learn to assign them bits and pieces of bigger assignments. This way, you are not left doing entire huge projects all by yourself. This can work in the home too. Delegate chores and household tasks to members of the family. They should all be playing a part!

CHAPTER 3. FOCUS ON THINGS THAT NEED DOING NOW.

Our brains have become attuned to distractions, so much so that it makes us feel great when we are distracted. Multitasking is a skill many of us have been taught, but we fail to realize that it drastically reduces our levels of intelligence. Multitasking leads to mistakes that could easily be avoided if we were to focus on a sole task.

When it boils down to becoming more productive, you don't necessarily need constant focus, but rather short bursts of distraction-free time.

TIPS TO BECOMING MORE FOCUSED

PERFORM CREATIVE WORK FIRST

We typically lean towards doing mindless tasks first to build ourselves up to conquer the tough tasks of the day. But in reality, this is draining your focus and energy. To effectively focus, learn to reverse the order. Perform the things that require you to use your concentrated creativity first, then start checking of the mindless things.

Deliberately Assign Time

It's been proven that the average person is only genuinely focused a mere six hours per week. Isn't this insane? Most folks tend to work best either in the morning or the late evening hours.

Pay attention to where you do your best focusing, and assign your toughest tasks to be done in these moments.

Train Your Mind

We have been taught to multitask, which makes us lose crucial focus and enables distractions to take over. With multitasking, you are essentially training your brain to be unfocused. Learn to consciously practice concentration by turning off any devices and paying attention to one task at a time. I recommend starting small; think five minutes per day, working up to larger amounts of time. Treat your brain like any other muscle in your body. It takes time to become fit, which means it takes time to build your brain to remain focused.

Challenge yourself by doing the following:

- Pick a task you wish to complete or needs to be done.

- Set a timer for 20-25 minutes.

- Work on that specific task and only that task till the timer goes off.

- Then take a 3-5 minute break.

- Continue this cycle till your task is completed!

CHAPTER 4. TELL PEOPLE YOUR GOALS AND BECOME ACCOUNTABLE

Goals are the lights to your potential path to success. Goal setting is not just a task you do, but rather an art form, one that many people are not fond of or great at.

One of the essential aspects of setting goals is learning to share them. This is what makes your goals visible.

BENEFITS OF SHARING GOALS

Accountability

When you share what your goals are with others, you are fueling the muscle of accountability. When you inform people in your life of what you want to do, you will be more likely to do them, since in the future they will ask!

Clarity

When you share your goals, you are more likely to mold them into what they need to be for your success. From one discussion to the next about your goals, new goals will emerge. Goals are initially shaped by interactions with others. The more you talk about them, the clearer and more structured your goals will become.

Measure of Progress

As you are taking leaps and bounds towards your goal, sharing your goals helps you to measure your overall progress in a better form. Don't feel afraid to use your peers and/or supervisors as guides. There is no shame in having someone you trust cheer you for your steps towards achieving something!

Motivation

Informing people of your goals acts as an incentive into actually fulfilling them. You don't want to disappoint people in your life, so discussing your aspirations with them is a great motivator.

Connection

Telling those that are like-minded about your goals helps to grow your social circle and make it stronger. Sharing something similar with another helps you to perform even the tiniest of actions towards your personal goal, which in turn creates a strong bond.

WHY ACCOUNTABILITY HELPS ACCOMPLISH GOALS

Accountability fuels the motivation we need to pursue the goals we want to achieve. If no one is around to inquire about your progress, then you are more likely to push it off until the following day. This is a dangerous cycle that will leave you stuck in the same rut.

Accountability also plays a powerful role in creating crucial social connections with others. It allows us to receive positive reinforcement, which fuels us with the motivation we need to power through.

More often than not, accountability provides adequate meaning to the core of our goals. Posting and sharing your goals with others helps you not to lose track of what you are doing it in the first place. It keeps the passion alive, which enables the positive action to remain intact.

CHAPTER 5. DO THE OPPOSITE TO WHAT YOU NORMALLY DO

"If you always do what you've always done, you'll always get what you've always got." –Henry Ford

All of us as humans have established methods of doing both simple and complicated tasks. We brush our teeth with a certain hand, we write one particular way, etc. But going out of your way to perform even these simple everyday tasks differently can greatly improve your willpower because it is far more difficult than we realize.

The fact of the matter is, through our struggles we find and acquire the understanding of what it is like to live with discipline.

Self-discipline is not only limited to money and material things but rather how we orientate ourselves in life. Disciple, thankfully, is a habit that can be learned and implemented.

Doing things in a different manner, such as developing a new morning routine, jogging on a different pathway, eating a contemporary meal, etc. can help you to remain focused on the tasks of everyday life. It enables us to remain motivated to be healthy, active, and consciously aware of the world around us and the part we play in it.

CHAPTER 6. SURROUND YOURSELF WITH POSITIVE PEOPLE.

The people who are in our lives play a vital role in our overall success. You are the average of the five individuals you spend the most time around. With that fact in mind, maybe it's time to peer into your life and take a good look at who is in your life and who effects it in positive and negative ways.

WHO DO YOU SPEND THE MOST TIME WITH?

Take a few moments to think about the folks that you spend quality time with. Then, write down their qualities.

- Are they happy, positive people?

- Do they make you feel like you can achieve your goals?

- Do they support you in what you do and wish to do?

- Do they make you feel important? Attractive? Etc.

- After spending time with them, how do they make you feel? Energized? Happy?

LEARNING WHAT 'GOOD' MEANS TO YOU

Everyone is different, meaning what makes you happy may not make them happy. Your ideas will differ from that of others. The sweet spot is locating the individuals that are *good* for *you*!

Keep in mind that 'like attracts the like.' What does this mean? When you give off good, positive vibes, these are the people and things you will ultimately attract in your life. This will attract those that are genuinely right for you directly to you, and weed those that don't have your best interest in mind out.

Surrounding yourself with good people fuels the ability to be surrounded by a good life. Good folks eliminate stress and bring you joy in the everyday things. I challenge you to commit yourself by beginning to spend time with those individuals that bring you happiness and motivation to achieve your goals!

TYPES OF PEOPLE TO SURROUND YOURSELF WITH

Many factors lead to success. While motivation and hard work are necessary, improvement to yourself can be massively driven by other people.

Those that we hang around most often impact the way we feel, act, and think. The only way you are going to better yourself is to engulf yourself in the presence of people who push you to better yourself. Here are the types of people that positively impact lives:

RELENTLESS WORKERS

Many people know at least one individual in their life that works hard and also pushes people to do the same. It's easier to measure your personal drive through the drive of these folks. Commitment and passion breed success.

Positive Attitudes

It's no secret that those who are happy with what they do are way better at their life's work than those that are not fulfilled by it. Negative minds drag your work ethic down and offer no inspiration for innovation. Negativity is the downfall of creativity, which positive people have the exact opposite effect. Positivity keeps morals high, and people constantly motivated to make the best better.

Inquiring Minds

"The most important thing is to not stop questioning." – Albert Einstein

Successful people are never afraid to ask questions. People who inquire are fueled by curiosities and have a desire to fulfill them. We also learn valuable information from those that ask questions, which can lead to a new mindset or train of thought. Inquirers are the people that lead people to breakthroughs for success and change perspectives.

Dreamers

Don't get yourself confused with people who have their heads in the clouds all day but do nothing to act upon their dreams. Truly successful dreams understand the importance of setting goals and putting in the hard work to achieve them. They like the challenge of achieving the unachievable. This is why surrounding yourself with these folks will provide you that touch of inspiration you might need to keep moving forward.

You are the sum of who you spend your valuable time in this lifetime with. Ensure that you are involved with people who will help you drive your success, motivating and inspiring you to be the best version of yourself you can be!

Chapter 7. Make short Term Achievable Goals.

When people think about setting goals, they only consider laying out long-term ones. While these are awesome, they are often far away, which makes it hard to know when to start and how to begin achieving them. This is the reason many long-term aspirations remain dreams that never become fulfilled.

That is why short-term goals are so pertinent to success, for they provide us with the perfect solution to what we struggle with in regards to long-term goals. Short-term ambitions offer us milestones that pave the path for achieving long-term goals. They provide clarity to our everyday lives.

Benefits of Short Term Goals

- Provide achievability and motivation to attain goals

- Minimizes procrastination with a path of clear, defined goals

Learning How to Make Your Goals *SMART*

For goals to be effective, they must be specific. They need to be aggressive but achievable. Use the SMART guidelines to ensure that you have the capability of setting adequate goals that will lead you to success!

- **S**pecific: Answer *how much and what kind*

- **M**easurable: Must have quantifiable terms, or they will become merely intentions.

- **A**ttainable: Inspires you to aim higher. Set goals around what you know you can achieve.

- **R**esponsible: Goals are assigned to you, meaning you are responsible for the success or failure of implementing them.

- **T**ime specific: Always add a timeline to follow so that you have an idea of the time allotted to accomplish them.

HOW SHORT-TERM GOALS LEAD TO LONG-TERM SUCCESS

There is research to back up the fact that if you **put your goals in physical writing**, that you are more likely to put action to them. Writing your aspirations out holds you accountable.

Advancing your career and knowledge isn't only about landing yourself in a higher-up position. Rather, it's about becoming better at the job you already have. This can be done by taking a step into what you want your future to look like and committing to **learning something new each and every day**. Learning these new skills and having that initiative to expand your knowledge helps build the foundation for success.

Obstacles are inevitable, and we can easily lose track of the bigger picture when trying to figure out how in the world to jump over hurdles. Instead of pondering over what could go wrong, **focus on a solution**. If there's a will, there's a way, and the willpower to move ahead despite obstacles will help you power through and pave your way to success.

To become more successful, you must be **willing to put in the work to hone your skills and learn brand new ones** that will aid in moving you up.

As you venture into the world of short-term goal creation, you will find **that altering the route to where you want to go becomes something that you have to be okay and comfortable with doing**. This is why remaining open to new worlds of possibilities will be your ally.

CHAPTER 8. REMEMBER THE 'WHY.'

Every person on Planet Earth has a 'why,' even if they have yet to truly discover what it is. What *IS* a why? It's the purpose, cause, or believe that inspires and motivates you. Knowing your personal why gives you the ability to make choices in all aspects of your life that will help you to find greater fulfillment in *everything* you do!

Your 'why' becomes the greatest joy that gets you up bright and early in the morning. It provides clarity to what matter most in each and every day.

I wish I could tell you that there was just one clear pathway to finding out your life's purpose, but sadly it's not that simple. Fortunately, there are a plethora of ways that you can dig inside yourself to view life on a larger scale and figure out what you have to offer the world.

Take genuine time to reflect on the following questions. You will hopefully find your sweet spot that resides within the intersections of what you are passionate about, what you have to contribute, and what is valuable.

QUESTIONS TO FIND YOUR 'WHY'

WHAT BREATHES LIFE INTO YOUR LIFE?

Before you dive into what inspires you and make you feel alive, I am not referring to dreams. Think bigger! Think about the why that lies beneath being about you to being something larger than yourself. Think about your passions. Connecting with them will help you to focus your attention on those specific endeavors that light up your mind, heart, and soul. This is what will truly influence and provide impact.

What are your elemental strengths?

What makes up our 'element' is the point in which our God-given talents meet with passion. When people reside in their element, they are productive and can provide value to their lives and to the lives of others. These folks also tend to make more money by doing what they love!

What are things you are good at? Are you good at being able to see complex patterns? Are you naturally creative? Are you a rebel with the capability to know where makeovers need to be done in regards to the status quo? Are you brilliant in regards to details? Are you gifted with communication? Are you a natural born leader?

This doesn't mean that you have to only be passionate about things you have talents in. Just keep in mind that it is rare to aspire toward ambitions that we don't have natural talents for.

Where is your greatest value needed most?

You can be awesome at a certain task but absolutely hate it. This will not bring you any fulfillment in life. That is why realizing what your strengths are and knowing how and where they will add the most value is essential to success. This is the only way you will find a great sense of accomplishment in contributing to the world.

We tend to undervalue our expertise, skills, and strength. This is why you should reframe the idea of adding value by solving issues, but rather think about where your skills would be better used to solve things in regards to a bigger picture. This will lead you to success in focusing on your natural strengths.

How will you measure your life?

Those that fail to stand for something tend to fall for anything. Making a stand helps you decide how you will measure your life's work and keep you aligned with what you were meant to do.

Living with a purpose is important to hone in on the things that matter the most. The most vital things are not "things" at all. Realizing and sticking to your purpose will compel you to take on hurdles that will stretch what you know and inspire you to be better.

Chapter 9. Learn How to Manage Stress.

Stress is hard on us both physically and mentally. Stress is an inevitable aspect of life, but it's up to you in how you let it impact your life. You can dwell on it and drown, or you can overcome stress with powerful resolution. To stay on track to success, it's crucial that you learn tools and techniques that will help you from falling victim to this unpleasant ailment.

Stress greatly impacts our ability to do our jobs, how we work alongside others, our relationships, careers, and more. This isn't even mentioning the physical conditions that can originate from letting stress overtake your life.

To properly manage stress, you must understand where those stressful feeling are born from. As an individual who has suffered greatly from stress-produced anxiety, I highly recommend keeping a stress diary. Jot down what events, thoughts, situations, etc. lead to feeling stressed. Then, list those stressors in order of the impact they have on you and your life.

Now that you have those written our to physically see, it's time to learn about these successful approaches to manage stress. You don't want all that hard work on building your willpower to be washed away by stress, do you?

Action Approaches

Managing Time

The amount of work that is piling up on that to-do list can easily be a cause for stress, especially if you don't know how to manage your time well.

- Create a to-do list and prioritize the list from important to not as important.

- Focus on one task at a time.

- Learn to do a lot with small allotments of time. Take the 5-minute challenge. What small things can you accomplish in 5 minutes?

- Avoid multitasking, turn off devices, etc.

People Stressors

As we are all too aware, people can be a great source of stress. Make sure that you spend time with people that positively impact your life and try to spend less time with folks that do the opposite.

Environment

The space in which you function and work in can be a place of discomfort, frustration, and irritation. It's important to minimize stressors in your working environment(s):

- Stress typically derives from:

    o   Poor lighting

    o   Loud noises

    o   Unhealthy air

    o   Overcrowded workstations

- o Crowded commutes

- o Uncomfortable conditions

- o Cluttered workspace

While these things may be not quite of an issue in the grand scheme of things, adding them together and eliminating them can help you to have a much less stressful workplace.

EMOTION APPROACHES

These approaches are most helpful when dealing with the way you view and perceive a situation. Negative thinking is a common cause of unnecessary stress.

- Utilize and practice positive thinking on a regular basis

  - o Smile more

  - o Surround yourself with positive individuals

  - o Change negative tone of thoughts to positive

  - o Take responsibility for your life

  - o Help someone in need

  - o Sing

  - o Think of 5 things you are grateful for

- Create a positive affirmation that you can mentally repeat within yourself when things are stressful, or you become wildly irritated.

- Utilize visualization/meditation to calm yourself and get yourself into a relaxed state of mind.

Acceptance Approaches

These approaches can be applied to situations where you can't change the course of what occurs. To build yourself up to protect yourself from stress:

- Utilize meditation and relaxation techniques

- Use your "support network," which is made up of family, friends, co-workers, etc.

- Ensure that you are getting adequate sleep and exercise

- Learn ways to cope with changes to build resilience so that you can properly overcome setbacks when they happen.

Stress occurs when we feel threatened, and we strongly think that we do not have the power or resources to deal with challenging scenarios. Look into the crucial priorities in your life. Learn how to utilize time management skills to your advantage. Learn to block out negativity and become a positive thinking and doer.

Simple Ways to Ease Stress

Here are some easy ways to relieve yourself from becoming overly stressed out wherever you are!

- Make a game plan: To-do lists reduce stress and give you the ability to remain focused.

- Deep breathes: At times, take a step back and allow yourself to take a few deep breaths. This will allow your body to get into a relaxing mode.

- Scale it down: You must set realistic expectations to become successful, conquer the world, and lead a fulfilling life. If you set expectations that are too high, you will become overly stressed in trying to achieve them.

- Know the signs: Know the physical and mental signs of stress, such as headaches, fatigue, negative thoughts, irritability, etc.

- Create a budget: We all know too well that finances are a big cause of stress. Living alongside a thought-out budget will help you from spending too much and becoming stressed about it in the future.

- Eat and drink smart: Eating a well-balanced diet will help you to manage stress levels much better than gorging on junk foods and filling yourself with alcoholic beverages.

- Laughter is the best medicine: No, literally! Stress levels are greatly reduced when we laugh and smile.

- Chat it up: Those who feel they don't have another person to turn to are more apt to feel the weight of stress more than those that can confide in someone they trust.

- Listen to your favorite jam: Listening to soothing tunes or music you like can help your blood-pressure levels drop to a better state.

- Exercise: Exercise has the power to release those feel-good hormones that help us to feel happier.

- Sleep tight: Those that don't get adequate amounts of rest tend to be less tolerant of stressful situations.

- Confront stresses: Ignoring stress can only get you so far. You must learn to confront it to prevent ailments like depression and anxiety

CHAPTER 10. OVERCOMING ROADBLOCKS.

"Just as we develop our physical muscles through overcoming opposition – such as lifting weights – we develop our character muscles by overcoming challenges and adversity." – Stephen Covey

Like you have read previously, challenges are inevitable in life. Right when you are cruising along at a good speed, BAM, they strike. People feel that life is hard simply because they don't have a plan to put into action when adversity strikes.

Life does this funny thing to us, making us persevere and learn from bad times in our life. There is a standard that all of us could learn from that involves the four states of mind: Spiritual, Emotional, Physical, and Mental.

A unique way of looking at your life as a whole, bad situations included, it so look at the dimensions of wellbeing:

- Physical

- Intellectual

- Occupational

- Environmental

- Spiritual

- Emotional

- Social

All of the above play a valuable part in our overall life. They each play a part in how we think and react. Learning about each of these puts you a step ahead of most in overcoming the roadblocks of life, powering through and becoming a stronger person. This chapter will break down each of those parts and also establish steps to get you conquering those pesky roadblocks!

INTELLECTUAL

Every day you have a choice on how you control yourself and your thoughts. That's why it's vital to think like a champion, *every single day*. This is easier said than done since the roller-coaster of life can drop us into traps and make us believe we are undeserving of our goals and aspirations.

You must practice beginning each day with truly believing that you are capable of great things! This helps you to always have a hunger for knowledge and a thirst to succeed. Successful intellect requires anticipation; the expectation that the next great thing in your life transforms directly from your thoughts and actions.

Physical

You must take care of your physical well-being to be successful in life. You can't go achieve dreams when you are constantly exhausted. You can't expect to fuel a powerful mind with Twinkies. What you put in your body is essentially what you are going to get out of life in the long run.

Social

Building and maintaining transformative relationships will help you in achieving the things you are capable of and more! Start with immediate connections and branch out from there, investing in those you work with, go to school with, etc. It's important to show and tell people you care. Don't be shy about this. Once you have established good relations within your immediate circle, expand it and interact with like-minded folks in your community. As humans, we are social creatures who are meant to grow with others.

Occupational

Wellness in regards to your occupation is finding fulfillment in the job you do every day. Many folks live highly unfocused and unhappy lives in the matter of their work. The secret to finding happiness is to take the risk to increase your tolerance for risks.

Think about it; the world has a funny way of providing us with what we ask for. If you want to open a bookstore, guess what? It WILL happen if you start the steps to working towards that dream.

Emotional

Emotional wellness and intelligence is a broad topic, but in regards to honing your willpower, don't take rejection personally. It's inevitable that at some point in life, you will be disappointed and rejected. It happens!

Instead of becoming overly anxious about challenging emotions, you need to feel them out. The more you understand the way you feel, the better chance you can grow from things and enhance your levels of emotional intelligence.

Love and joy are impactful emotions that can spread like wildfire. Make it a priority to tell someone in your life that you love them. Humans always enjoy the feeling of being accepted and treasured. I recommend keeping a personal journal of your thoughts and emotions, this way they are easy to track and you can look back on them. You will soon see that being consciously aware of the emotions we naturally feel can help you to regain equilibrium in your emotional life!

Spiritual

You only have the power to control what you can. You need to accept that some things in life will always be out of your hands. What are your values? Taking your core beliefs and utilizing them to determine your actions can make a huge difference in staying on a path to success and becoming lost on the road to nowhere.

You must learn how to cultivate faith not only within other people but also within yourself. You must believe in yourself first to get in touch with the things that you *can* control. Know what you are capable of, what you are not, and come to peace with it. You can then adequately build the foundation of your life around your values.

Environmental

What are you doing each day to make the world a better place to swell? While you are the only person who can decide and act upon things to pave your road for success, never forget that your actions should provide some sort of value to that of others. What are the results of how you act and what values drive you to act the way you do? I picture actions like ripples within a pond. Even those that just get the tail-end of your ripples will be affected in some way.

CHAPTER 11. PRACTICE MINDFULNESS MEDITATION.

While the thought of meditation may seem like a complicated concept, it really is simple! All you have to do is find a comfy place to sit, be attentive to your breathing, let your mind wander away and return to you. This chapter will lead you through the exact steps of how to practice mindful meditation!

STEPS FOR SUCCESSFUL MINDFUL MEDITATION

First, find a good area in your home that isn't cluttered and is quiet. You can leave the lights on or sit in the natural sunlight, whichever you choose. If you desire, you can even sit outdoors, just be sure to pick a place that won't be distracting.

(If you are a beginner to meditation, I recommend starting with just 5-10 minutes and gradually working all the way up to 45-minute meditation sessions. Many folks perform meditation both in the morning and in the evening, or one of the two. Better to perform this at least once a day than not at all!)

Once you have found a spot to meditate peacefully, your next step is being consciously aware of *how* you are sitting. Here is a posture practice in which you will find success in stabilizing yourself if you only have a few moments to relax.

- Ensure that you are sitting in a stable spot.

- Take notice of what your legs do. If you are sitting on the floor, cross them in front of you. If you are sitting in a chair, make sure the bottom of both your feet makes contact with the floor.

- Straighten your body, but let your spine sit in a natural position. Do not force or stiffen your upper body. Your shoulders and head should be comfortably resting on your top vertebrae.

- Place your upper arms parallel to your torso. Allow your hands to drop to your sides or upon your legs gently.

- Drop your chin down a bit and allow your gaze to fall downward. You can also allow your eyelids to rest a bit too, or you may close them entirely, although this is not necessary to meditate.

- Relax and pay attention to your breath, entering and exiting your body. Become aware of all your bodily sensations.

- Follow your breath and draw your attention to the physical sensation of breathing.

- Eventually, your attention will leave how you are breathing and allow your brain to wander. Don't attempt to block your train of thought. Take note of where your mind wanders. Within the meditation timeline you have allotted, return your attention back to your breathing.

- Pause before attempting to move. Remember to shift at moments you choose, letting the space between you and your experience in.

- Don't worry if you find that your brain seems to be running at 100-mph, this is normal, especially when you first start out. Instead of fighting and engaging in those thoughts, practice the action of observing without reaction.

- When you are ready, lift your gaze gently and open your eyes if you have them closed. Take note of the sounds around you. Also really pay attention to how your body feels, what your brain is thinking and how you feel emotionally.

- That's it! You have successfully practiced a meditation session! Relaxing, right?

CHAPTER 12. SELF-AFFIRMATION.

Without failure, success in life would not be possible. Mistakes are constant reminders that we are not perfect, but inform us of the things we could do better. They bring out and make clear of the qualities that make us uniquely who we are as individuals. In a nutshell, this is what self-affirmation is. It's all about learning to preserve out self-worth even in the face of shortcomings.

Positive self-affirmation has been shown to minimize stress, anxiety, and defensiveness that comes with the things that threaten our sense of self. But how in the *world* does the self-affirmation process actually work in terms of willpower?

Self-affirmation, in a scientific sense, has been proven to make us more open to feedback and threats, which in turn make us more emotionally receptive to the errors we inevitably make.

Affirming your core values boosts your overall willpower. How? By providing self-control, even when it's wildly depleted. Self-affirmation acts as a mental strategy that reduces the likelihood of failure caused by lack of self-control.

SELF-AFFIRMATION EXERCISE

To exercise self-affirmation does not mean that you must repeat weird mantras like 'I'm the best' constantly to yourself. It's about becoming consciously aware of your core values. A good exercise to start with would be to write your list of core values and then write a paragraph or two about their value to you and your life. Here is a sample list:

- Meaning of your life

- Changing the world

- Health

- Teaching others

- Helping others, friends, family, etc.

- Career

- Family

Remember that self-affirmation doesn't necessarily have to be related to the areas in your life that you are looking to improve. Just write your values out and recall moments in which you successfully utilized them.

STEPS TO MAKE AFFIRMATIONS WORK FOR YOU

Step 1: Create a list of what you think to be your negative qualities. Think about criticisms and other similar things. Don't think too hard about if they are accurate. While doing step 1, remember that you are human, and having flaws is part of our natural beauty. Now that you made a list take a strong look at a recurring theme. Maybe these negative afflictions scream at you that *you are unworthy*. Finding a theme is a fantastic place to start in changing your life for the better and building a strong foundation for willpower.

Step 2: Jot down affirmations that relate to your positive aspects. I would recommend dusting off a thesaurus and finding powerful words. For example, instead of simply stating you are *worthy*, try words like *cherished* and *remarkable*!

Step 3: Ensure you are saying, seeing, or thinking your affirmation(s). Say the affirmation out loud for 2-5 minutes, three times a day. State it out loud during your morning routine, amidst your lunch break, and before you hit the hay. You can also write our this affirmation multiple times in a notebook, or even write them on sticky notes that you can stick around the areas in your life you live within the most.

Step 4: Learn to anchor those affirmations within your physical self by placing a hand on areas that feel uncomfortable when you wrote them out previously. Learn the importance of breathing in and taking in those affirmations. This will help you to reprogram your mind and mold those conceptual affirmations into reality.

Step 5: Accountability! Get someone you trust to repeat the affirmation to you. This works really well with a close loved one or spouse. You can then pick the affirmations and lift one another up each day! If you do not have someone in your life you trust with your affirmations, take some time in front of the mirror each day and repeat it to yourself. Sounds silly, but makes a *world* of difference!

CHAPTER 13. GET A GOOD SLEEP ROUTINE.

Adequate amounts of quality sleep can make a big impact on our overall wellbeing. Sleep helps our physical selves heal, allows our minds to rest and recharge, and boosts our abilities to conquer the next day.

Here are just a few reasons why quality sleep is vital to everyday life:

- Prevents us from eating too many calories that accelerate weight gain

- Improves productivity and concentration levels

- Maximizes physical performance

- Lessens risk of stroke and heart disease

- Lessens risk of developing diabetes

- Lessens risk of developing depression

- Improves the immune system

- Decreases inflammation in the body

- Directly affects how we interact with people and react to situations

Sleep quite literally is part of the core to successful living. If you are one that struggles to get an adequate night's rest, then this chapter can do wonders in boosting your levels of willpower!

Getting a Better Night's Sleep

Getting in Sync with Your Body's Natural Cycle

Our body has a natural sleep-wake cycle, also known as the circadian rhythm. If you strive to stick to a regular schedule, your sleep-wake cycle will be easier to sync up to and help you fall asleep faster, achieve better sleep, and wake refreshed.

- Go to bed at the same time every night. This informs your body's built-in clock that it's time for rest.

- Don't sleep in. Yes, that means even on those peaceful weekends when your schedule is clear. The more you vary your schedule, the harder it is to achieve quality sleep.

- Nap smart. If you are one that has issues falling and staying asleep, that nap that sounds good can make your problems worse when it comes time to go to bed.

- Fight drowsiness after dinner-time. If you manage to get tired before it's time for bed, do something that stimulates you, such as cleaning dishes, getting clothes ready for the following day, talking to a friend, etc.

Control Exposure to Light

Our bodies naturally produce melatonin, which is directly controlled by our exposure to light. Your brain knows to secret melatonin when it's dark, which makes you sleepy. Spend more time out in the sun during the day, and learn to avoid staring at device screens 1-2 hours before you lay down.

Exercise Daily

Exercise plays a part in boosting levels of metabolism, rising core temperature, and stimulating hormones. This means you should avoid exercising close to bedtime. Make sure to finish your workout at least three hours before you plan to lay down.

Be Smart About What You Consume

Your eating habits during the day can wreak major havoc on your quality of sleep.

- Limit nicotine and caffeine

- Avoid eating big meals in the evening

- Don't drink alcoholic beverages before bed

- Avoid drinking too much liquid before bedtime

- Cut back or avoid consuming sugary eats and refined carbohydrates before bed

Learn the Importance of Winding Down

We have all been there, our braining running faster than our car can make it down a freeway, *right* when we are trying to go to sleep. Anger, worry, and the daily stress can make it challenging to get to sleep.

- Learn to look at life in a more positive perspective. This can help you to wind down at night.

- Learn stress management skills to keep the stress of everyday life at bay.

- The more you overstimulate your mind during the day, the more difficult it can be to settle the mind at night. In today's world, we are practically taught to overstimulate ourselves. Through the constant checking of social media, emails, phone calls and more, it's no wonder we have issues focusing on one task at a time.

Practice Relaxation Techniques

Performing techniques that help you relax before bed is a sure-fire way to calm your mind and prepare your body for sleep.

- Deep breathing: Close your eyes. Take deep, slow breaths, making sure each breath is deeper than the last.

- Muscle relaxation: Begin with your toes, tensing the muscles in your feet tightly, and then relaxing them. Continue this with all of the muscle groups in your body.

- Visualization: Shut your eyes and imagine yourself in a place that is peaceful. Concentrate solely on how being in that place makes you feel.

Other Relaxation Bedtime Rituals

- Dim your lights

- Perform simple preparations for the next day before heading to bed. Less you have to worry about!

- Get your favorite books on tape and listen to them

- Perform easy stretches

- Perform favorite hobby before bed

- Listen to soft music

- Enjoy a warm bath

- Read a magazine or book in a softened light

Learn Methods to Get Back to Sleep

It's normal to wake up during the night. Here are some great tips to help you get back to sleep:

- Stay out of your head by concentrating on how your body feels practicing deep breathing exercises.

- Make relaxing a priority, not sleep. The harder you try to get some shut-eye, the more challenging it is to fall back asleep.

- Perform a stimulating, quiet activity

- Put off brainstorming and worrying for tomorrow

CHAPTER 14. TRY NOT TO DRINK SO MUCH.

Alcohol has been shown to impair willpower and self-control. While a drink or two on occasion is certainly not a bad thing, alcohol is one of those substances that are best consumed in careful moderation.

Alcohol is infamous for reducing our overall self-control, and it wildly alters our mental state of mind. It inhibits our mental capacity and the ability to establish and utilize willpower. Many people assume that alcohol is responsible for people doing dumb and destructive things. But in fact, it's alcohol's ability to erase restraints.

Consuming alcohol has a funny way of affects behaviors directly related to inner conflicts. Long story short, if you are looking to strengthen your levels of willpower to change your life and become successful, alcohol should be avoided or at least carefully consumed.

Chapter 15. Make it easier to succeed than to fail.

Succeeding is better than failing, there is no secret in that. But what could you be doing differently to ensure that you will be successful? This chapter outlines just that!

Making it Easier to Achieve Success

Micro Habits

These types of habits are simple changes that can be made with ease. Fine tuning the smallest of everyday behaviors can make a huge difference in the long run. To bring micro-habits into perspective, picture the habit as oil and gas within your car. If they are on their own, they are quite useless. But getting to your destination successfully takes the using both of them.

Intentions

Intentions are designed to be similar to resolutions and goals, but they are more complex than micro-habits. This means they change less frequently as well. Intentions are created within a specific plan of action and help us to track progress within bigger projects in our life.

Success Statement

This layer of ensuring success is a personal one. You are the only one responsible for the actions that drive your fulfillment and success. So, what are the steps you need to take to make yourself prosperous? Your ideas of success will mold over time, changing as you become your authentic self. You will learn to focus on your sense of purpose.

Essence Statement

This statement is built from your values, which can be difficult to pinpoint. Learn to choose core beliefs that clearly represent your philosophy of life as a whole. This can change over time as well, especially depending on events that happen.

As you live your life, you will inevitably have to make extremely complex decisions. That's where the essence statement comes into play! It can help you to locate your sense of direction. When you take the time to sketch out your key beliefs, you will have a clearer mind and will be better able to move forward despite complex situations.

Habits of Successful People

If you wish to become more productive in your life, start implementing these habits that many fruitful individuals use on a daily basis:

- Wake up earlier: Waking up at an earlier time allows you to think about the day ahead, unplug for a bit, and track time. During these hours there should be no expectation other than mentally preparing yourself to deal with the usual chaos of the day.

- Keep promises: No matter how mundane or significant, strive to keep the promises you make. Talk, especially in today's world, is quite cheap. Actions will always speak volumes compared to words alone. The foundation of success is built on the trusting relationships we create.

- Learn how to tell a good story: This starts all the way at the bottom of the totem pole, with your interview. You need to learn ways of talking that make an impact and speak to people so that they remember you.

- Don't dictate: There is a huge difference between being a leader and merely being a boss. Learn to walk right alongside your employees instead of dictating their actions.

- Embrace failure: Without failure, no success could be born. Don't be afraid or embarrassed of failing. Instead, embrace it! You never know what good could come from it.

- Never be afraid to inquire: To raise the possibility of new angles and perspectives, you must learn the importance of asking questions and *a lot* of them.

- Be honest: Don't only be honest with those in your life, but with yourself as well. If you learn to live beside a lie inside, it will show in your ability to achieve success.

- Breaks are vital: Unplugging is always a good thing! Everyone needs a breather from time to time. It can do wonders in helping you to stay sane and help you refocus on your goals.

- Take notes: Part of staying organized in life is learning to take notes. Our brains are complex, so looking back at those "pointless" notes later can raise questions that can further you to reaching the sky!

Chapter 16. Better Exercises and Nutrition.

When faced with the challenge of eating healthier and taking better care of our bodies, willpower is the one thing that keeps us from constantly hitting snooze, going on that early morning jog, taking us to the gym, and avoiding those tempting vending machines at the workplace. But did you know that taking better care of yourself physically can strengthen willpower? Being healthy and gaining control over your life go hand in hand.

Willpower and Health

We all have experienced cravings. Making healthy food choices can literally mean the difference between gaining weight and developing related diseases or remaining healthy. It often boils down to the willpower we have. Willpower rises and falls all the time, which is a good reason to keep that in mind when you are faced with the challenge of eating an apple or leaning towards that donut.

The Rise and Fall of Willpower

The following are reasons that our levels of willpower fluctuate in relation to health:

- Willpower decreases when you don't get at least 6-7 hours of sleep: While lack of sleep can make you naturally crabby, it also causes your hormones to regulate weird, which can make your appetite fluctuate. This is why those that don't get enough sleep often opt for sugar and greasy eats.

- Willpower increases when you are feeling great about yourself: Willpower is obviously going to be the strongest when you wake up in a good mood, feel good about yourself mentally and physically and are ready to conquer the day. Willpower is fueled by our emotional resources. That's why we have a lack thereof when we feel angered or sad.

- Willpower increases when you eat good foods: Your body can break down the things you consume easier if they consist of natural proteins, fibers, and vitamins. The less your body has to do, the more energy you have! This is why eating foods that are loaded with carbs and sugars literally weigh you down in more way than one.

- Willpower is lessened from taking care of your children: When you are focused on your kids and their activities, you fail to focus on yourself. It's easy to do, as every parent knows. Children naturally leave you feeling burnt out, which can lead to terrible eating choices.

- Willpower decreases when you are overloaded with stress: When you are under tons of stress, your body naturally releases hormones to help you handle it all. But along with those hormones comes those pesky craving for foods that aren't so good for you. Stress weakens willpower, which means you are less likely to plan ahead, which can result in making bad food choices.

Easy Ways to Ensure Better Food Choices

Even though our willpower is better on some days in others regarding the decisions we make in what we fuel our bodies with, here are some easy-to-implement daily tips to ensure you are eating the best things possible!

- Cut back on the consumption of foods high in calories

- Truly know what you are consuming. Take time to read the labels on products before throwing them in the cart.

- Simplify! Opt for food choices that are natural or close to their natural state.

- Be realistic. If you are craving something like ice cream, grabbing a giant handful of carrot sticks is probably not going to satisfy that craving. Instead, opt for something like Greek yogurt with berries or perhaps a frozen banana.

- Learn to plan. It's much easier to make healthy choices if they are already planned out ahead of time. Pack lunches, plan out snacks, etc. Focus on replacing those bad eating habits with better ones while you are creating your plan.

CHAPTER 17. ENJOY THE CHILL TIME.

On occasion, you should take a time out from everyday life, enjoy it and learn the importance of planning time to relax! It's just as crucial as working hard, if not more so. It's all about finding a nice balance between work and play.

Don't believe me? Take a look at these relaxation benefits:

BENEFITS OF RELAXATION

- Protects your vital organ, the heart. Stress can increase health risks, such as heart attacks and high blood pressure. Stress can be easily compared to a lack of healthy eating, hypertension, and lack of exercise.

- Lowers the risk of catching common ailments. No one likes enduring a cold, but the less time you take to relax, the more apt you are to get colds, flu, and other sicknesses. This is because stress alters our body's natural defense system.

- Boosts memory. Stress that exists for long periods of time has a way of impairing out the prefrontal cortex, which can negatively impact our memories. It also plays a part in increasing the risk of developing diseases such as Alzheimer's, dementia, and others.

- A safety net from depression. Stress literally kills off brain cells and prevents the creation of new ones. This can inhibit the hippocampus, the area of the brain that is responsible for producing healthy responses to stress, to act appropriately.

- Aids in better decision making. It's no secret that enduring stress can inhibit our ability to make good decisions. It can cloud our judgment when it comes to weighing the option of reward and risk.

- Helps you keep fit. Stressed folks tend to opt for those calorie-packed comfort foods, which can pack on the pounds in a short amount of time.

- Decreases acne. Stress causes our skin to produce excess oils, which is a direct cause of acne. It clogs pores and results in flare-ups, usually at the most inconvenient times.

- Increased sexual drive. Stress, as many of us are aware, greatly inhibits our ability to get and stay "in the mood." Stress lowers libido in both sexes.

WAYS TO RELAX IN JUST 5 MINUTES

When there are 50+ emails lining your inbox, people bothering you non-stop at work, screaming kids, keeping track of the activities of those you love, etc., it can be hard to think about relaxing and making time for it. Here are a few great methods of relaxing that take 5 minutes or less:

- Drink green tea: Green tea has L-Theanine in it, which helps to relieve anger.

- Nibble on dark chocolate: Regulates stress hormones and stabilizes your metabolism.

- Consume honey: Made up of compounds that decrease inflammation within the brain.

- Eat a mango: Has linalool, a compound that aids in lowering stress levels.

- Meditate: We have discussed the positivity of adding meditation to your daily routine previously! Take just 5 minutes to find a quiet place and chill.

- Take slow, deep breaths.

- Count backward: When your mind is running faster than your dream car, count to ten and work your way back.

- Utilize visualization: Perform 'creative visualization,' which is practically regular visualization, but rather like mini daydreams that instill happiness in your stressful environment.

- Use a golf ball: Make sure to have a golf ball with you at work. Rubbing your feet back and forth against a golf ball provides a relaxing foot massage!

- Get alone time: Sometimes, many people need only a few moments along to clear their head and de-stress a bit.

- Spend time out in the sun.

- Stare out the window: Find a nearby window and lose your current thoughts to the environment outdoors.

- Organize your living and work space.

- Get up and stretch

- Write it out: When you feel stressed, turn to your diary. Putting emotions out on paper can make them less stressful and intimidating.

- Listen to your favorite music and don't forget to dance!

Ways to Unwind in 60 Seconds

- Stare at the ceiling and count down from 60. Counting deliberately will help you to avoid distractions.

- Write out any worries or concerns in a designated notebook and set them aside for the next day.

- Inhale through your nose and exhale through your mouth ten times.

- Picture yourself on a cloud, floating. What do you see passing by? This is a powerful mindful meditation tool!

- Tense and relax muscle groups all over your body.

Chapter 18. Make your 'TO DO' list manageable.

For those to-do lists to really work for you in regards to achieving success and building willpower, you need to realize that there are right *and* wrong ways to make and utilize them.

This chapter outlines great tips to keep your to-do lists in check and make them work for you instead of against you!

Tips for Successful To-Do Lists

Pick a Good Medium

You need to ensure that your to-do list can be accessed with ease. Whether it's just a tiny notepad that resides on your desk or an application on a mobile device, make sure that it really works for you and your personal preferences.

Make It Visible

Make sure you leave your to-do list(s) in places that you can easily view them throughout the day. This will enforce that sense of urgency you need to get things done.

Begin Each Day with a To-Do List

Make it a habit of sitting down and writing out what you need to do at the start of each and every day. This is the most optimum time to plan your day since your mind is at its freshest.

Make Lists One Day at a Time

Don't attempt to plan your entire week ahead. Hone in on the tasks that need to be accomplished at the end of each day. This will help you to focus on priorities rather than get lost in the hustle and bustle of the week in its entirety.

Write Important Tasks at the Top

Ensure that you jot out the most crucial things at the top of your to-do list. This way, you can tackle the things on that list in order. Otherwise, what's the point of a to-do list?

List the Things You Are Supposed to Avoid, Too

While it may sound counteractive, writing out the things you are supposed to avoid can help you keep on track and not lose focus and productivity.

Make the Number of Tasks Reasonable

Don't add absolutely everything that comes to mind to your list of things to get done. Make sure you are realistic when it comes to the number of things you put down on your to-do list.

Take Breaks

Breaks are important to remain productive throughout the day and cross off everything on your to-do list. Finish tasks before taking breaks, but make sure to try to take a breather between tasks.

Put Uncompleted Tasks on the Next Day's List

It's okay if you don't get everything done that you have written down, just stick it on tomorrow's list! No need to sweat!

CHAPTER 19. GET YOUR BIG TASKS DONE FIRST.

The bigger the project, the more intimidating it tends to be, which is why we like to procrastinate and put off larger tasks and work on small and build our way up. But this is not the most efficient method of getting things completed.

Make sure to look at the day's tasks adequately. I recommend to always begin with the tasks that have the closer due date if they possess one.

Brainstorm how long you think tasks will take. If you don't think you can accomplish them in a day's time, perhaps break them down into a number of smaller tasks to successfully fulfill them.

FOCUS: THE SECRET TO PRODUCTIVITY

The capability to focus on one thing and one thing only is much easier said than done. But focus is the ultimate secret to being productive!

I have personally learned the positive effects of scheduling off time to truly hone in on conquering larger tasks. This means you may have to work on just one task, but through the breakdown of creating it into smaller chunks.

Avoid distractions. This means you will have to avoid social media, silence your cellular device(s). This will help you gain and sustain the momentum you need to nail that task on the head!

If you decide to tackle all these small tasks first in an attempt to avoid those bigger ones, you are wasting precious brainpower and energy on those when you can be utilizing that focus to get more crucial things done.

CHAPTER 20. DEVELOP SMALL BUT IMPORTANT HABITS.

One of the issues I find in interacting with folks in everyday life is the fact that we deal with so many impactful, large things, we tend to forget where they originated from. The most successful people in the world today all had to start from scratch somewhere. But we all have goals and dreams and try to locate the fastest route to achieving them. This is the wrong way of thinking.

The greatest things start very small, which is why even the smallest of chances and habits can have a huge impact on your life over time. When you make things smaller, you are actually more likely to succeed. No one can change the world overnight, but baby steps towards a specific goal of changing the planet in mind can land you just where you want to be.

We are creatures of habit, which means our habits, from small to big, have a good say in dictating who we are and who we are capable of becoming.

In the spirit of willpower, here are just a few of the best habits to implement and have in your life:

- Wake up earlier

- Take the time to think about and express gratitude every day

- Smile and laugh more frequently!

- Eat healthy meals, but especially breakfast

- Drink water with a squirt of two of lemon to boost your immune system. You can't change the world if you are always sick, right?

- Make time to exercise every day

- Make it a goal to walk 10,000 steps per day

- Consume adequate amounts of vitamins and minerals

- Have and utilize effective time management skills

- Make goals each day

- Learn the importance of inspiring yourself to make the best better

- Learn to save and invest for the future

- Learn the vitality of learning new things daily

- Organize all aspects of your life

- Contribute to the lives of others

- Don't wait; take action *today*

- Make a plan and learn the steps to following it through

- Utilize positive thinking as often as possible!

Chapter 21. Make Plans. Short-term *and* Long-term.

To really get to where we want to in life, we must prioritize the process of making plans and setting goals to fulfill those plans. This involves the creation of short and long-term plans, not just one or the other. Plans and willpower go hand in hand in the fact that they aid us in staying the course of who we want to become over time.

Ways to Increase Your Success with Short and Long-Term Plans

Goals can be classified into the categories of short and long-term, obviously. Short-term goals are typically ones that you can achieve in 6 months to a year's time, while long-term goals take anywhere from 3-5 years to accomplish. You must learn how to properly set up short-term goals to enable you to successfully reach your long-term ones.

Make Goals Specific

Everyone wants to be successful, I mean, who *doesn't*? But what does the word success mean to you specifically? Learn what defines being successful for you and your life before attempting to make goals.

Have the Ability to Measure the Outcome

When you are creating goals to achieve, you need to set a time frame in which you are to accomplish them. This way, you set yourself up for success and not an automatic failure.

Scratch Out Negativity

Don't start out in a negative state of mind right from the get-go when sitting down to plan your goals. Instead, think of it in a sunshine-y light! You don't want to be stuck at that dead-end job for years? Then how can you improve your skills to land that dream job?

Make Goals Realistic

Ensure that you have the skills and abilities to reach those long-term goals. You can't go out and win a Grammy Award if you have never recorded a song, for example.

Tie Actions to Your Goals

If you wish to graduate college with your bachelor's degree, then the action tied to this goal should be something like complete the credits that are required to obtain it.

Keep Goals Flexible

There are bound to be barriers that stand between you and your long-term goals. But this doesn't mean to give up on them! Remember that setting goals will not guarantee that you will be successful, but they raise the odds that you will come out with the gold!

CONCLUSION

Congrats! You made it to the end of *Willpower!*

Each chapter in this book discusses specific aspects of developing a better sense of willpower, learning to utilize self-control and create a discipline for you to follow. If you read the book in its entirety, you should now have a nice boost of confidence that you do indeed have what it takes to become successful in your career and personal life!

Willpower is the element in life that keeps us as human beings walking forward in the face of adversity and hardship. Without it, we would not be where we are today as a civilization!

I hope you found this book valuable, useful, and helpful in discovering parts of yourself that you didn't know existed. Through self-discovery and developing a stronger sense of willpower, you will have a better chance of locating your life's purpose, as well as opportunities that best suite you and your vision. Good luck!

OTHER BOOKS BY APOSTLES GRADALES

Emotional intelligence. 21 steps to master your emotions and improve your relationships.

Building Confidence: 21 steps to overcome self doubt and social anxiety.

ONE LAST THING...

If you enjoyed this book or found it useful, I'd be very grateful if you'd post a short review on Amazon. Your support really does make a difference, and I read all the reviews personally so I can get your feedback and make this book even better.

If you'd like to leave a review, then all you need to do is click the review link on this book's page on Amazon here:

Amazon.com/review

Amazon.co.uk/review

Thanks again for your support!

Printed in the USA
CPSIA information can be obtained
at www.ICGtesting.com
LVHW011015210724
786093LV00031B/1027